Transportation, Links, and the Local Community

Dr (Er) Om Prakash

Professor & Chairman (T&P)

SMS Lucknow:

Table of Contents

1.0 Introduction

2.0 Feasibility Study of Extending The Docklands Light Railway (DLR)

2.1 Introduction

The Docklands Light Railway was initiated in the 1980s to expand the mobility of a growing region of the Docklands in London. However, as the economic viability of the region improved, especially with the introduction of the Asian business Port (ABP), there has been a growing need for the expansion of the DLR. This section of the paper will discuss the feasibility of the extension of the DLR. A feasibility study of the extension of the DLR from Becton to the Fenchurch Street line, near to barking, serves to find out exactly how achievable it is to complete this project. To determine the feasibility of this project, it is necessary to cover certain crucial aspects of the proposed extension plan. These issues include the technological, legal, operational, economic, technical, schedule, and financial aspects of the project. These are the key elements of the project that will showcase just how well the project is prepared for the numerous hurdles that might come up during implementation.

2.2 Technology and System Feasibility

The modern railway system is increasingly becoming sophisticated, and thus the need for incorporating technological elements in the system to aid in managing it. From the onset, when designing, developing, and initiating the use of the railway, technology will be used in many ways. The advantage here is that there are many other similar projects that have been implemented around the world. This means that it is possible to borrow solutions from other such projects. Another factor that makes this project feasible in a technological and system perspective, is the advance in technological field within the railway industry. With increased railway traffic around the UK, the use of computer-aided systems to manage the system has become necessary. The same systems could be used to provide the extension of the DLR with a plausible implementation. Because of these facts, it is possible to conclude that the extension of the DLR is possible on a technological and system point of view.

2.3 Legal Feasibility

The legal aspect of a project is as crucial as any other part, as the legality of a project could result in delays that could derail the project. Aspects of the project that require legal streamlining include the staffing, sustainability, and land allocation. When it comes to staffing, the extension of the DLR will create many jobs. However, when employing workers, it becomes necessary to ensure that the right steps are followed in employing and remunerating the employees. It also becomes necessary to follow all the rules and regulations in that govern the employment of workers. The sustainability of the project is also under constant legal checks from relevant stakeholders. If the project is deemed unsustainable with regards to maintaining the environment as well as the society surrounding the project, the law can be used to stall the project. The land to be used for the project can also bring in legal issues if it is not obtained appropriately. This project is deemed feasible on a legal perspective because of the fact that all the stakeholders, including the government, are working together to ensure that all the legal structures are followed to the letter in the expansion of the DLR.

2.4 Operational Feasibility

An operational feasibility study of the expansion of the DLR serves to examine how well the project satisfies the needs of the ABP. By serving the needs of the ABP, the project will be found feasible on an operational perspective. However, the project also needs to fit into the current structures that are already in place. These structures are the current DLR system as well as the economic infrastructure. The expansion of the DLR to the Fenchurch Street line from Becton will serve to increase the mobility of people and goods to and from the ABP. This fits in with the current economic infrastructure in that it enhances the financial flow of goods and services for the businesses surrounding the intended extension of the DLR. The extension of the DLR will also ease the transportation problems for people from Becton to the Fenchurch Street line. The people using the line will not have to be operating into the ABP. This goes to show just how this project is operationally feasible.

2.5 Economic Feasibility

The economical implications of the expansion of the DLR are particularly big. The reason behind this is the huge cost incurred during the development of the project as well as the implementation. However, it is important to point out that after the completion of the project, the economic benefits will far outweigh the costs incurred during implementation. Some of the economic benefits that will arise from the implementation of the expansion include increased mobility, and reduction in the need for the use of roads. This is economically important because the costs of moving people and products will be reduced. Reduction of these cost increases the avenues with which these finances can be used. The extension of the DLR will also reduce the time of commuting between Becton and the Fenchurch Street line. By increasing the speed by which products are availed to their destination, time is saved, and thus increasing the flow of money in the economy around the extension.

2.6 Technical Feasibility

The technical aspect of the extension of the project is particularly important because it enhances the confidence of those using the DLR in the project. Technology is a big part of the extension. To develop the DLR between Becton and the Fenchurch Street line, technology will be important. This is because certain aspects such as measurements between one area of the DLR to the next cannot afford any room of error. The expansion of the DLR will employ contractors that are experienced in the developing similar railway lines. This implies that the extension is particularly feasible on a technical perspective. Advanced technology will ensure that the final product that is the extended DLR will fully serve its purpose as well as fit in with the increasing demands of the new project.

2.7 Schedule Feasibility

The schedule feasibility serves to identify whether the extension of the DLR will fit in with the final opening of the ABP. If the project time schedule is not particularly feasible with regards with the overall time schedule, then it will become difficult for the overall goals of the entire project to be achieved. The reasoning behind this is that if the extension of the ABP takes too long, then the project may become unreasonably slow. In a project like this, time is particularly essential. The extension of the DLR is particularly small in comparison to other similar projects. The legal aspect of the extension has already been sorted out, making the implementation process even easier. The contractor expected to work on the project have been found to have an impeccable record of accomplishment. This means that the chances that they will go off schedule are minimal. These facts show that the schedule of the implementation of the project is particularly feasible.

2.8 Financial Feasibility

The financial feasibility study of the extension of the DLR provides details of exactly how the project will be financed and whether the money availed will be appropriate for the project. The ABP has set aside £1 billion for the entire project. The extension of the DLR has been considered in the amount mentioned. From the money set aside for the extension of the ABP, some will be used for remunerating all the stakeholders involved in the extension. Another amount will be used in ensuring liquidity during the implementation stage. This will ensure that the final project is not facing sudden costs that it cannot finance. The financial feasibility of the project clearly shows that with proper planning for the finances set aside for the project, the end goal of completing the project in time will be achieved as expected.

2.9 Conclusion

The extension of the DLR from Becton to the Fenchurch Street line will introduce new opportunities to the people as well as the businesses in the said region. The end result is that many people will benefit from the creation of jobs as well as the opening up new trade routes. However, the feasibility study of the entire project is necessary to determine whether the project will be beneficial in the end. To determine the feasibility of this project, many aspects of the project have been discussed. The study has revealed that the project is feasible. All the stakeholders involved the project need to work together to ensure that project does not fail during the implementation. Upon completion, the benefits will be immense. The people who will rip from these benefits are the members of the society as well as the businesses in the area.

3.0 Comprehensive Plan For Extending and Linking Transport Networks to ABP

3.1 Introduction

The main routes to the proposed Asian Business Port within the Royal Albert Dock are via air (planes), rail, sea, and road. These means of transportation converge on the proposed site for the business port in a manner that will allow for future expansion of the business port. Currently, the roads and other transportation infrastructure are not linked and extended to the proposed site. However, for the effective use of the new port that is set to be completed by the year 2017, a comprehensive plan is needed. This raises the need for a research in to the various routes, problems the extensions will solve, the goals of the extensions, means for collecting data for this plan, how to prepare for the plan, and the implementation of the plan. This section of the paper will delve into identifying the key steps followed into ensuring the success of the transportation puzzle in and out of the proposed Asian Business Port.

3.2 Main Routes to ABP

The routes to the Asian Business port consist of routes via the dock itself (river), the railway line, air (Heathrow airport), and by road (Royal Albert Way). The extension of various routes to connect these main ways into the proposed ABP will help in reducing the issues faced when moving from other locations within London to the ABP. One such extension is the extension of the DLR from Becton to the Fenchurch Street Line. All the other routes will also be modified to increase accessibility to the proposed site. To make the Abp a success, it is important to ensure that the port is accessible. The plan is to extend the main routes used to access the proposed business port to make it even easier to get to the port.

3.3 Problem Statement

The problem currently is that all the routes to the proposed site are only capable of allowing transportation of people and their goods at a smaller capacity than the expected movement by the completion of the port. To alleviate this situation, the transportation routes to the port need to be modified. The DLR needs to be extended; the roads to the Royal Albert way from the ABP need to be expanded; the docks to the river near the ABP also need to be modified. This will go a long way in ensuring that the overall goal of enhanced transportation to and from the ABP. Enhancing the transportation means to and from the ABP ensure that those working from the port can move rather easily. It also ensures that the goods transported into the port arrive safely. This is particularly crucial for the business people working in the port, the property owners in the ABP, the workers in the ABP, as well as access for social amenities.

3.4 Goals

The main goal is to ensure that the Abp is easily and efficiently accessible. To achieve this goal, the main routes to and from the ABP need to be modified. This requires the cooperation between the various stakeholders involved in this project. The government and the company ABP have come into agreement and the Asian company has set aside £1 billion for the project. The first extension will be that of the DLR to bring it closer to the ABP. This will provide means of transport from the ABP to the rest of London for those working and living within the port. As for the roads, there will be an increase in traffic to the area. This will introduce a need for the expansion current highways in the region and the creation of new roads to the ABP. This should ease the traffic to and from the port. The other goal is to modify the port for ease of access from the river. This will increase the amount of goods that can be brought into the port.

3.5 Data Collection

Data collection ensures that the planning process is precise. Data collection is important whenever a project is being implemented, it allows one to make strategic decisions based on facts. To collect data for the extension of transportation facilities within and around the ABP, it will be required that the planning body identifies the key transportation mechanisms in the area. These are road, water, and rail. This means that the transportation body needs to liaise with the ports, roads, and railway authorities. The mayor has appropriated all the facilities within the local government that will ensure that the process of collecting data from the relevant transportation authorities is possible.

3.6 Plan Preparation

A first step towards the plan preparation is to identify all the tasks required to achieve the object and goals as defined for the project. All the tasks required to ensure that the ABP is easily and efficiently accessible, need to be categorized. Each category of the tasks can be further divided into sub-tasks within the category and which can be further drilled-down to individual activity. It was highlighted earlier that to achieve the goal, the main routes to and from the ABP need to be modified. This requires the cooperation between the various stakeholders involved in this project. So as a next step in plan preparation, all the main routes must be identified and this step constitutes a major category of the task. The identification of the needs to modify the routes to achieve the object of this project constitutes the activities within the task.

As is generally required in preparation of a project plan, each task and its activities must be assigned a time-line. The time-line itself has several variables like expected start time, duration and expected time of completion. It is mandatory to break-down each activity with respect to the timelines as described above, if a standard methodology of project management is to be followed. Usually, the trend in modern construction and infrastructure project is to follow the standard project management methodology. Therefore, the plan preparation also requires developing a project network diagram and activity network diagram which clearly illustrates the sequence of the activities.

This helps in optimizing the project implementation as this assists the Project Manager and the project teams to start certain activities in parallel. Thus, with respect to the current project the plan can be prepared to start certain tasks and activities in parallel so that the main routes to and from the ABP could be modified optimally. As this is one of the huge construction projects, so the plan preparation should be such that a slack or a buffer period needs to be maintained, so that if one activity gets delayed, due to unavailability of a resource or other such similar constraint, then the complete project duration or timelines may not suffer.

To optimize the overall project target, which is to provide means of transport from the ABP to the rest of London for those working and living within the port, it is necessary to prepare a critical path to complete the project in an optimal duration. If the Critical Path Method (CPM) is followed, the chances are that the project will be completed well within the specified timelines and budget. So this is the importance and advantage of the professionally prepared project plan.

Stakeholder identification, project team creation and recruitments, if necessary, are the integral parts of this step. It is assumed that a skilled and experienced Project Manager would have already been identified as a first step towards the Project Team creation. Project Manager is the key personnel for the success of the project, so the incumbent must have the excellent levels of communication and team management skills, besides the domain knowledge of construction management. As an excellent and effective communicator, the Project Manager is required to drive the project, throughout the life-cycle of the project. So as a next step in the development and preparation of the project plan, it is of considerable importance that the communication plan is prepared and propagated effectively. It is through a proper communication plan that all the team meetings would be identified and organized along with the set frequency. Therefore, towards the success of this construction project, communication plan will ensure that all the key stakeholders are well informed about the happenings of the project, they are all aligned and are in same page. Other important tasks within the scope of plan preparation are risk identification and mitigation plans, work breakdown structure, organization structure and a category each for project completion and commissioning based activities, along with the timelines and budgetary information.

3.7 Plan Implementation

In one of the most critical activity in Project plan preparation is to allocate the budget, if possible, allocate a task wise budget. It is known that the government and the company ABP have come into agreement and the Asian company has set aside £1 billion for the project. So £1 billion is a rough estimate of the total project budget, and the plan can reflect this budgetary requirement in its cost accounting. So, obviously the first step towards the implementation for this project is to get the approvals of the budget from the project sponsors. It is known that the following decisions have been taken which can successfully kick-start the project implementation:

"The Mayor:

(a) APPROVES the Evaluation Panel's recommendation to select ABP (London) Investment Ltd as preferred bidder for the Royal Albert Dock site;

(b) APPROVES the closure of the procurement process and GLA Land & Property Ltd's entry into the Development Agreement ("DA") with ABP (London) Investment Ltd;

(c) DELEGATES to the Executive Director of Housing & Land and the Executive Director of Resources everything necessary or expedient to facilitate the implementation of this project, including the fine-tuning and execution of the DA and any ancillary documentation;"

Thus, form the aforementioned decision, it is clear that the Executive Director of Housing & Land and the Executive Director of Resources is to act as the Project sponsor for this project, acting on the behalf of the Mayor. It is further assumed that all the budgetary approvals and amendments thereof need to be taken by the Executive Director. Once the budget is approved, the project implementation can kick-start with the first set of activities as planned per the project plan, as devised in the previous section. Presently, the Project Management Software like Microsoft Project Manager can be used to enter the project plan, activities, Project Schedules, Project Network Diagram, Work Breakdown structure, Team structure, roles and responsibilities of each team members, budget and cost accounting, contingency plan, project slack, and host of similar other activities. As best practices adopted for the major construction management project, the Project Manager, and other stakeholders of the project like to record the daily log of activities. They have an access to the interface or screen which leads them to current status and details of the project, wherein they can choose a link to record the daily logs. The software helps to record actual, like actual finish date of a particular activity and helps to ascertain whether the project is on track and is within the anticipated timelines and within the budget.

Since, the risk assessment and mitigation plan is also entered, it helps the team members to act as per the mitigation plan, whenever an anticipated risk confronts the project team. This helps in the smooth operation and implementation of the project. Therefore, it is assumed that all such plans, activities and schedules would be appropriately entered and maintained with the selected project management software like Microsoft Project Manager, which has the capability to provide for the adherence of the advanced standards in construction management projects.

3.8 Alternatives Evaluation

It is a standard and accepted method to furnish the alternative strategies for implementing the construction projects. Risk mitigation, resource constraint and budgetary restrictions entail the development of alternative methodologies and recourse to the project tasks. An important object of the project is that the main routes to and from the ABP need to be modified. In-depth analyses of the best possible identification of the modification needs may reveal a couple of alternative methods in achieving the same object. One strategy is to minimize the risks in implementing of the changes to the routes. This means the there would be minimum friction and impediments in developing the new routes from the stakeholders or the parties who may be affected under such developments. (GLA, 2013)However, mitigation or minimization of risk may be concomitant with the extra time or resources required to accomplish the new changes. Hence another alternative solution could be to adopt a critical path method or the shortest path in the development, although it may require a better risk management plan and intervention of stakeholders and project sponsor in the even if the risk arise while the implementation.

Conventionally, up to three candidate solutions can be proposed and it is for the Project Board to approve and adopt a particular solution. The actual implementation of the project is dependent on the adoption of such solution. But, before that the Project Board may oblige the consultant teams to evaluate each of the candidate solution and propose the pros and cons of each solution and propose the recommendations. Benefits of each solution can then be evaluated along with the related risks and the capacity of the Project sponsor or the board and the general preparedness to work under the related risks, of a particular solution is adopted. If the risks are too high, then a better solution can be adopted, even if it means, rising of the budget to meet the extra costs as entailed by the solution.

3.9 Plan Adoption

Plan adoption implicitly assumes the adoption of a candidate solution in the construction management project. Once a solution is adopted, it signifies that a respective plan which is typical to the solution is also adopted. This plan may have its specific project schedules, specific work breakdown structure, team roles and responsibilities, budget and activity wise cost accounting and the risk mitigation plan. Once the plan is adopted, the specific amendments are made in the project management templates, and the project kick-off meeting can signal the start of the project as per the adopted plan. Project Management software can be effectively utilized from this stage for all the activities related to the project, as from this stage the actual plan implementation would be required to be followed as per the plan adopted.

3.10 Monitoring of Plan During Implementation

In the construction management project, where a lot of workers in the team could be sub-contractors, it is a recommended best practice to closely monitor all the activities of the plan, record a daily log in the project management interface and allow the role based access to the interface to all the project team members and stakeholders. It is assumed that for this large scale construction management project, all the details are deftly entered in the software. As a first step, a project profile must be created and shared with all the team members so that the details entered by one member is immediately available, at least in a read only (non editable) mode to all other members.

One crucial advantage of monitoring and administering all the details online is that all the team members are aligned towards the current developments and the team is also aware as to what is expected from them from time to time. Due to the availability of work breakdown structure, the teams are aware well in advance that what they are supposed to do next. Communication plan, which records all the requirements of team or stakeholder meetings are also in place, along with the frequency and schedule. This helps to set-up an automatic reminder which enables the required team member to be alerted well in advance about the important meeting scheduled along with the date and time. Regular communication and team meetings are key to success as it helps to share the important updates with all the required team members instantaneously and ensure that all the doubts and questions of the team members or stakeholders are addressed adequately within such team meetings.

The interface also provides for recording the minutes of the meetings, the action plan, and helps to review the action plan in the next such meeting. Thus, this is the best way to monitor the activities of the project and help to evaluate instantaneously the status of the project and whether the project is within the track and within the allocated timelines and budgetary allocations. Risk management plan helps to alert the respective teams of the impending risk and reminds about the risk mitigation strategy. This helps the stakeholders to monitor whether the project is currently under some risks and whether such risks have been sufficiently tackled or mitigated adequately.

3.11 Conclusion

This section began with determining that the main routes to the proposed Asian Business Port within the Royal Albert Dock were via air (planes), rail, sea, and road. These means of transportation converge to the proposed site for the business port in a manner that would allow for future expansion of the business port. The goal was to ensure that the ABP is easily and efficiently accessible, and for which candidate solutions are proposed to be developed, taking into account the budgetary allocation, adherence to the timelines and mitigation of risks. It was highlighted that in such high level construction projects, risk assessment is necessary as it can be major show stopper for the project. A suitable solution and plan is adopted by the Project Board and the implementation of the project is dependent on such adoption. It was recommended that the extensive use of project management software to be made in order to ensure the smooth functioning of the project. All the major tasks and activities can be optimally managed and monitored through the effective use of the interface provided.

4.0 Report on Carbon Emissions and Journey times from ABP to London Bridge

4.1 Introduction

As major step towards community development and corporate social responsibility (CSR), t eh companies today are aware about the impact they make towards the deterioration of environment due to their typical operations. There is conspicuous presence of a commitment to reduce the carbon emissions and thereby reducing the impact or carbon footprint they make for the sustainable development of construction industry. ABP, for instance, has been consistently collecting the data to carbon emissions from the year 2002 onwards. The port has shown its commitment towards the reduction of carbon footprint and managing its resources to achieve this goal. Earlier section highlighted the alternative routes possible to travel to and from ABP within the Royal Albert Dock, that is, via air (planes), rail, sea, and road. It is very well known that the lowest carbon foot-print is presented by the travel mode of rail. (ASSOCIATED BRITISH PORTS, 2014)

4.2 Direct Emissions

The direct emissions are the Scope 1 emissions, which are from the sources directly owned by either ABP or the Docks. This classification is as per the GHG Protocol of emissions (UNCW, 2011). The Climate change Act mandates the reduction of greenhouse gas emissions and adapt to climate changes. In summary, the Act mandates the following of standards for emission reduction, setting the targets for reduction and maintains the charts, which help to monitor such reduction on annual basis. Direct emissions include the emission of Carbon dioxide and other such gasses, collectively known as Green House Gas emissions (GHGs), which affect the state of the environment. The below figure shows the nature UK transports greenhouse gas emissions, 1990-2009: (Department of Transport, UK, 2014)

As evident from the below figure, the direct emissions from the aviation industry is highest, where there is no appearance of emissions from the railways. Therefore, the direct emissions from the Rail are lowest, and their contribution towards the carbon footprint is just through the indirect emissions, as it operates through electricity (Networkrail, 2014).

4.3 Indirect Emissions from Electricity Purchases

These emissions are known as the Scope 2 emissions. Indirect emissions are from sources which are neither owned by ABP or Docks, but, are linked to the electricity energy consumption. Purchased electricity is the example of such consumption.

4.4 Indirect Emissions from Transportation Emissions

These are the Scope 3 emissions under the GHG Protocol of emissions. Scope 3 emissions are other sources that are neither owned nor operated by ABP or Docks but are either directly financed (i.e. commercial air travel paid by ABP or Docks, waste removal) or are otherwise linked to the campus via influence or encouragement (i.e. air travel for study abroad programs, daily faculty, staff, and student commuting). Emissions associated with paper consumption and landscaping activities are included in this Field.

As per Dr. Melissa M. Bilec (Greenhouase Gas Inventory division), "emissions that fall under Scopes 1 and 2 are mandatory and must be included in the inventory by the

GHG protocol. Although Scope 3 emissions are deemed optional by the GHG protocol, researchers are encouraged to include as many emission sources as possible to obtain a realistic inventory for the institution." (Dr Bilec, 2013) Therefore, it will be mandatory for the ABP and the Docks to maintain the records of direct and indirect emission as described under Scope 1 and Scope 2 above.

4.5 Journey Times From ABP to London Bridge

A train from London Bridge Station to Albert dock takes about 3hrs 13 minute. A bus route takes around 5 hours and 34 minutes for the same source and destinations as shown in the below diagram. As an alternative means of transport to London docks, there is London Cable Car, also known as Emirates Airline – which is a cable car which crosses River Thames in East London, between The Royal Docks near Canning Town and the Greenwich Peninsula. A single trip costs £4.30, with a journey time of 5 minutes and can seat up

10 people and keep to bicycles. This service is being effectively used by the staff of the docks. The Royal Docks Terminal, on the north side, is close to the Excel Centre. The Greenwich Peninsula Terminal, on the south side, is close to the O2 Arena.

Source: Tripadvisor: http://www.tripadvisor.in/Travel-g186338-c180036/London:United-Kingdom:London.Cable.Car.html

Source: http://www.rome2rio.com/s/London-Bridge-Station/Albert-Dock

4.6 Conclusion

Rail or cable car offers the lowest carbon footprint, whereas the shipping or aviation contributes highest towards the direct or indirect carbon emissions. Companies, like ABP have started realizing the importance of reducing the carbon footprint and have started contributing towards the CSR activities and community development programs. The importance of using bicycles and cable car was highlighted which can ease out the problem of emissions and reduce the carbon footprint. The initiative seems to be successful as the service is being actively used by the employees and the staff. Since the potential of the project will create lot of extra jobs, this service can be effectively utilized by the staff. This can substantially reduce the number of busses and cars moving to and from the port.

5.0 Engineering Solution for a Bridge and/or Tunnel

5.1 Introduction

A new container port at the site would mean massive traffic loads on the Waterside road and rail links, with major effects also on the nearby residents (Lewis, 2000). This may further result into a danger of huge and unsightly installations, like container stacks and this may also pose a risk to damage natural environment, especially caused by the traffic congestions. Basically, there are three ways in which the extra traffic burden can be avoided – constructing a bridge over the Southampton Water or constructing a tunnel below it. A third way could be to off-load containers from ships at Dibden Bay directly onto barges for ferrying across the water.

5.2 Problem Statement

A decision to construct a new container port at the site can result in huge traffic congestion and this would almost certainly have a deep impact on the environment. The load of this burden will also be shared by the nearby residents living in or around that region, a large portion of which is of the employees and staff which would be directly affected.

5.3 Suggested Solution

There could be possible three solutions to this problem. First solution is to construct a bridge over the over the Southampton Water. This would considerable ease out the traffic load. Second solution is to build a tunnel as an alternative, or could be built together with the bridge, if the situation so warrants. A decision can be taken to either build a tunnel or a bridge or both. However, building a bridge will not hamper in anyway, the construction of the tunnel in the future. As a third alternative, other way could be to off-load containers from ships at Dibden Bay directly onto barges for ferrying across the water.

5.4 Structural Test

The structural tests for bridges and tunnels are meant for testing static and dynamic wind loads. The bridge and tunnel stability analyses can be done through DVMFLOW simulations. The simulations also enable to test the girder flutter analyses which are necessary for the bridge girders. Considering the fact that the bridge and the tunnel would be subjected to heavy loads, proper stress tests as provided through the DVMFLOW (COWI, 2009) simulations and air dynamics tests would ensure the stability and safety of the bridge as well as the tunnel.

5.5 Conceptual framework (Theory)

Using the concept of pre-fabricated elements of the bridge and tunnel is the part of the accelerated construction framework (Administration, 2009). On many projects, construction of the bridges is the critical path to the overall completion of the project. This may not be the case for large roadway projects where there are few bridges. In the present case, as it was highlighted earlier, construction of the bridge and or tunnel can be a critical path in the project, which may affect the deliveries or affect the residents or the environment. Therefore, construction of the bridge or tunnel must be a part of the accelerated construction methodology using the pre-fabricated parts. Latest techniques enable the construction of such bridges or tunnels with an extra cost. As it was highlighted earlier, all such aspects are to be provided in the candidate solution, which includes the risk management and cost benefit analysis.

5.6 Conclusion

The decision to construct a bridge or tunnel or both is a strategic decision, which can help to resolve the multiple problems resulting from the strategy to add to the facility provided by the port. Adding a facility of new container port, for instance at the ABP site, can result in the risks of traffic congestion, environment effects and problems related with the nearby residents. While adding to the facility purely has an economic basis, mitigating the risks is more towards the technical solution, like adopting the accelerated construction strategy of prefabricated bridges or tunnel.

6.0 Final Conclusion

ABP's ambitious vision for the site has an economic basis as it would further bring forth the investments from abroad. This would also bring more development and benefits to local people by providing thousands of new jobs and enhancing the waterfront for people to enjoy. While this is true, but, as the port decides to add the facilities, suitable steps would be required to mitigate the risks. For instance, the addition should be as quick as possible, if the risks to the environment and inconvenience to the local people is high during the transition period. However, there could be budgetary constraints as providing fast, sustainable and reliable solution would come with a premium cost. Therefore, it is recommended that before embarking to a new solution, a proper project plan must be prepared, together with the candidate solutions. Through the effective communication plans, the project Board and sponsor can adopt the right solution after carefully analyzing the cost-benefits and returns and the risk management plans.

7.0 Bibliography

Bibliography

Administration, F. H. (2009). *Connection Details for Prefabricated Bridge Elements and Systems.* https://www.fhwa.dot.gov/bridge/prefab/if09010/report.pdf.

ASSOCIATED BRITISH PORTS. (2014). *CLIMATE CHANGE ADAPTATION REPORT* . HUMBER, HULL, IMMINGHAM AND SOUTHAMPTON HARBOUR AUTHORITIES .

COWI. (2009). *Bridge Aerodynamics.* http://www.cowi.com/menu/service/BridgeTunnelandMarineStructures/Bridges/bridge-dynamics/Aerodynamics/Documents/021-1700-016e_09a_Aerodynamics_low.pdf.

Department of Transport, UK. (2014). *UK transport greenhouse gas emissions* . http://assets.dft.gov.uk/statistics/series/energy-and-environment/climatechangefactsheets.pdf.

Dr Bilec, M. M. (2013). *Greenhouse Gas Inventory.* University of Pittsburgh .

GLA. (2013). *Royal Albert Dock: Update, Short-listing of developers & 2012-13 Budget.* Green London authority. http://www.london.gov.uk/sites/default/files/MD1007%20Royal%20Albert%20Dock%20PDF.pdf.

Lewis, J. (2000). *HE DIBDEN BAY CONTAINER PORT'.* http://www.julianlewis.net/essays-and-topics/2952:the-dibden-bay-container-port-23.

Networkrail. (2014). *Value and importance of rail freight.* networkrail.co.uk.

UNCW. (2011). *Greenhouse Gas Inventory* . http://sustain.appstate.edu/sites/sustain.appstate.edu/files/UNC_Wilmington_ghgreport.pdf.

www.ingramcontent.com/pod-product-compliance
Lightning Source LLC
LaVergne TN
LVHW041258150826
845673LV00008B/2644

* 9 7 9 8 8 9 6 1 0 2 6 0 1 *